MORE STORIES FROM THE
JATAKAS

All living creatures die to be born again, so the Hindus
believe. The Buddha was no exception. Legend has it that several
lifetimes as a Bodhisattva went into the making of the Buddha,
the Enlightened One.

The Bodhisattva came in many forms - man, monkey, deer,
elephant. Whatever his mortal body, he spread the message of justice
and wisdom, tempered with compassion. This wisdom -- the wisdom
of right thinking and right living--is preserved in the Jataka tales.

The Jataka tales, retold in this selection, will keep you amused
while they show you how good ultimately triumphs over evil.

Editor : **Anant Pai**

Title	*Script*	*Illustrations*
The Giant and the Dwarf	*Luis Fernandes*	*Souren Roy*
The Mouse Merchant	*Subba Rao*	*Chandrakant Rane*
The Magic Chant	*Meera Ugra*	*Ram Waeerkar*
The Priceless Gem	*Yagya Sharma*	*Ram Waeerkar*
Tales of Misers	*Luis Fernandes*	*Ram Waeerkar*

Cover

C. M. Vitankar   *Ram Waeerkar*

Cover Design
C. D. Rane

THE GIANT AND THE DWARF

IN ANCIENT INDIA THERE ONCE LIVED A DWARF.

COMICAL THOUGH HE LOOKED, HE WAS EXCEEDINGLY CLEVER. AND HE HAD ONE GREAT TALENT.

TWANG!

ZZAT!

THUD

HE WAS AN EXCELLENT ARCHER AND PEOPLE CALLED HIM LITTLE BOWMAN.

HEY, LOOK AT THAT LITTLE FELLOW!

HE LOOKS SO FUNNY.

WHERE ARE YOU GOING WITH THAT GREAT BIG BOW, GOOD SIR?

I AM GOING TO THE PALACE TO OFFER MY SERVICES TO THE KING. I AM AN ARCHER.

AN ARCHER?

HO HO HO!

BE CAREFUL, OR YOU MAY TAKE OFF WITH ONE OF THE ARROWS YOU SHOOT!

HE! HE! HE!

I CAN'T BLAME THEM. NO ONE BELIEVES THAT A PUNY FELLOW LIKE ME CAN HANDLE A BOW AND ARROW.

4

YOU WON'T FIND A BETTER ARCHER ANYWHERE.

AND WHO IS THAT FELLOW?

HE'S MY SERVANT.

WELL, GOOD ARCHERS ARE HARD TO COME BY THESE DAYS. WE'LL FIND YOU A PLACE HERE.

SO BHIMASENA ENTERED THE KING'S SERVICE.

THEN SOME DAYS LATER—

DID YOU SEND FOR ME, YOUR MAJESTY?

YES, BHIMASENA.

I HAVE A TASK FOR YOU. A FEROCIOUS TIGER IS TERRORISING MY PEOPLE.

NONE OF THE MEN I SENT TO SLAY HIM HAVE COME BACK. THEY MUST ALL BE DEAD.

NOW I WANT YOU TO TRACK DOWN THE BEAST AND DESTROY HIM.

WHATEVER YOU SAY, YOUR MAJESTY.

THE KING HAS COMMANDED ME TO KILL A FIERCE TIGER WHICH IS TERRORISING HIS PEOPLE.

WHAT ARE YOU WAITING FOR, THEN? GO RIGHT AWAY!

WHAT!

AREN'T YOU COMING? YOU PROMISED ME THAT YOU WOULD... YOU SAID...

YOU CAN'T DO THIS TO ME! I'M GOING BACK TO MY WEAVING!

KEEP CALM, BHIMASENA, KEER CALM.

YOU DON'T NEED AN ARCHER TO GET THAT TIGER. I'LL TELL YOU WHAT TO DO. LISTEN...

7

SOON, BHIMASENA SET OUT FOR THE VILLAGE WHERE THE TIGER HAD LAST BEEN SEEN.

WHEN HE GOT THERE —

FRIENDS, I AM A HUNTER. THE KING HAS SENT ME TO RID YOU OF THE TIGER.

BUT I NEED MEN TO FLUSH HIM OUT OF HIS LAIR. ONCE HE IS OUT IN THE OPEN, I'LL DO THE REST.

YOU CAN TAKE ALL THE ABLE-BODIED MEN OF THIS VILLAGE WITH YOU, MY LORD. WE WILL SEND WORD TO THE OTHER VILLAGES, TOO.

WHEN BHIMASENA FINALLY ENTERED THE FOREST, HE HAD SEVERAL HUNDRED VOLUNTEERS WITH HIM.

THE VILLAGERS SET UPON THE TIGER...

...AND BEAT HIM TO DEATH.

THEY'VE KILLED HIM. GOOD! NOW FOR THE SECOND PART OF THE PLAN.

PULLING OUT A CREEPER...

...HE RUSHED BACK TO THE VILLAGERS.

WHERE IS HE? WHERE IS HE?

?

12

LATER —

DO YOU STILL WANT TO GO BACK TO YOUR WEAVING, BHIMASENA?

THAT'S A SILLY QUESTION, LITTLE BOWMAN. I CAN'T IMAGINE HOW I EVER DID IT. AND FOR SO MANY YEARS!

WEAVING BASKETS! HA! HA! HA!

THE GIANT BECAME POPULAR AT THE COURT. THEN A FEW WEEKS LATER —

YOUR MAJESTY, WE CRAVE YOUR PROTECTION.

A WILD BUFFALO IS TERRORISING TRAVELLERS ON THE SOUTHERN ROAD. HE ATTACKS ANYONE WHO PASSES THAT WAY.

SEVERAL MEN HAVE LOST THEIR LIVES ALREADY.

DELIVER US FROM THIS VILE CREATURE, O KING.

THAT BUFFALO WON'T TROUBLE YOU MUCH LONGER.

BHIMASENA!

OH! OH!

GO AND SLAY THAT BEAST! IT SHOULD BE CHILD'S PLAY FOR YOU.

YES, YOUR MAJESTY.

A WILD BUFFALO CAN BE MORE DANGEROUS THAN A TIGER. I HOPE THE LITTLE BOWMAN DOESN'T LOSE HIS NERVE.

BUT WHEN HE TOLD THE DWARF OF HIS ASSIGNMENT—

IT SHOULDN'T BE A DIFFICULT TASK FOR YOU, BHIMASENA.

FOR ME! WHAT ARE YOU TRYING TO SAY? IF YOU THINK I AM GOING TO WRESTLE WITH WILD BUFFALOES YOU ARE MISTAKEN.

I'M NOT GOING TO ENDANGER MY LIFE BY DOING YOUR WORK FOR YOU! WE AGREED THAT YOU WOULD DO ALL THE WORK, DIDN'T WE?

NOBODY IS ASKING YOU TO ENDANGER YOUR LIFE, BHIMASENA.

DID YOU ENDANGER YOUR LIFE WHEN YOU WENT TO KILL THE TIGER?

AH! THE CREEPER TRICK! NOW WHY DIDN'T I THINK OF IT MYSELF?

WHEN BHIMASENA CAME BACK TO THE PALACE A FEW DAYS LATER, HE HAD THE DEAD BUFFALO WITH HIM.

SO YOU GOT HIM. DID YOU HAVE ANY TROUBLE?

BHIMASENA!

NOW WHAT'S THE MATTER WITH HIM?

OUR HERO IS BACK.

LOOK AT THE SIZE OF THAT BUFFALO!

WELCOME HOME, BHIMASENA! I AM INDEED FORTUNATE TO HAVE YOU IN MY SERVICE.

YOU SHALL BE WELL REWARDED FOR YOUR EFFORTS.

BHIMASENA BECAME EVEN MORE POPULAR. SEVERAL FEASTS WERE GIVEN IN HIS HONOUR.

TELL US HOW YOU KILLED THE BUFFALO, BHIMASENA.

OH, IT WAS NOTHING REALLY.

HE DID PUT UP A TERRIFIC FIGHT. THE EARTH SHOOK UNDER US AS WE STRUGGLED.

16

HE HAS BEEN AVOIDING ME EVER SINCE HE CAME BACK.

I'LL WAIT FOR HIM, HERE.

AH, THERE HE IS!

BHIMASENA!

YOU DON'T SEEM PLEASED TO SEE ME. WHAT'S THE MATTER?

LOOK, LITTLE BOWMAN, LET'S GET ONE THING STRAIGHT. I DON'T NEED YOU ANY MORE.

ALL RIGHT, YOU TAUGHT ME HOW TO DEAL WITH THE TIGER AND THE BUFFALO.

BUT WHAT IS SO GREAT ABOUT THAT, EH?

IF I HAD GIVEN IT SOME THOUGHT, I'M SURE I COULD HAVE COME UP WITH A SIMILAR, OR EVEN BETTER PLAN, MYSELF.

YOU HAVE SERVED YOUR PURPOSE. NOW LET US PART.

OH, SO THAT'S IT! SUCCESS HAS GONE TO HIS HEAD.

I ONLY HOPE IT DOES NOT LAND HIM INTO TROUBLE. ANYWAY, I'LL KEEP OUT OF HIS WAY FOR A WHILE.

19

LITTLE BOWMAN, THEREAFTER, KEPT OUT OF BHIMASENA'S WAY. BUT THE GIANT HARDLY MISSED HIM. HE NOW HAD SEVERAL FRIENDS, BOTH IN THE COURT...

...AND OUT OF IT. HE SPENT HIS DAYS IN EASE AND COMFORT.

THEN ONE DAY —

YOUR MAJESTY, WE ARE BEING ATTACKED!

THE KING OF THE NORTHERN KINGDOM IS ON HIS WAY HERE WITH A LARGE ARMY.

YOUR MAJESTY, A MESSAGE FROM THE ENEMY.

"SEND OUT YOUR CHAMPION TO FIGHT WITH OUR OWN OR SURRENDER."

WE SHALL FIGHT! WE SHALL UNLEASH THE MIGHTY BHIMASENA ON THEM!

AS BHIMASENA SWAGGERED OUT OF THE PALACE AND WALKED MAJESTICALLY TOWARDS THE WAR ELEPHANT WHICH WAS WAITING FOR HIM —

BHIMASENA!

BHIMASENA, YOU'LL NEED SOMEONE TO CARRY YOUR SPEAR, WON'T YOU? I'LL COME WITH YOU.

GO, BHIMASENA. CRUSH THEIR CHAMPION AND WIN LAURELS FOR YOURSELF AND OUR KINGDOM.

VICTORY TO BHIMASENA.

CROWDS CHEERED THE GIANT AS HE SET OUT TO MEET THE ENEMY.

THERE GOES BHIMASENA, THE GREAT!

DO YOU SEE WHAT A GREAT MAN I'VE BECOME?

YOU CAN IMAGINE THE HONOURS THEY'LL HEAP ON ME ON MY TRIUMPHANT RETURN!

WHY, THEY MIGHT EVEN WANT ME TO BECOME THEIR KING!

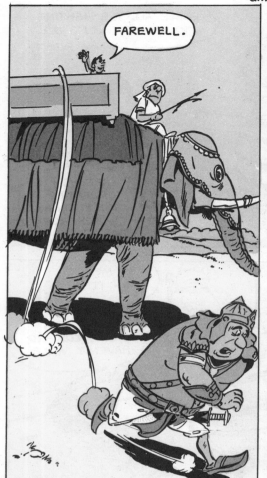

FAREWELL.

NOW TO COMPLETE THE TASK WHICH MY WORTHY FRIEND SET OUT TO DO.

IN THE ENEMY CAMP—

WHAT IS THAT LITTLE MAN UP TO?

?

IS HE THEIR CHAMPION?

WE SHALL SOON KNOW WHO HE IS.

LET HIM COME CLOSER. THEN I'LL...

ARRGH!

AS THE SOLDIERS AND THE ELEPHANTS RUSHED ABOUT IN A STATE OF PANIC, LITTLE BOWMAN CHARGED INTO THEIR MIDST...

...PULLED THE ENEMY KING OFF HIS ELEPHANT...

...AND SPED AWAY WITH HIS PRISONER.

SAVE ME! SAVE ME!

LATER—

YOU HAVE PERFORMED AN AMAZING FEAT, LITTLE BOWMAN. SINGLE-HANDED YOU HAVE CAPTURED THE ENEMY AND PUT HIS ARMY TO FLIGHT.

FROM NOW ON, YOU SHALL HAVE AN HONOURED POSITION IN MY COURT— BETTER EVEN THAN THAT WHICH WAS HELD BY THAT COWARDLY BHIMASENA.

LITTLE BOWMAN BECAME A GREAT HERO AND HIS FAME SPREAD FAR AND WIDE. AS FOR BHIMASENA, HE WAS NEVER HEARD OF AGAIN.

THE MOUSE MERCHANT

IN THE CITY OF VARANASI, A YOUNG MAN WAS ONCE ON THE LOOK-OUT FOR A JOB.

IT SO HAPPENED THAT THE ROYAL TREASURER, ACCOMPAINED BY A FRIEND, PASSED BY.

THE KING VALUES YOUR WORK. THE TREASURY IS OVERFLOWING WITH RICHES. WHAT IS THE SECRET OF YOUR SUCCESS?

INITIATIVE AND ENTERPRISE.

I'LL EXPLAIN WHAT I MEAN. DO YOU SEE THAT DEAD MOUSE?

YES... BUT....

EVEN IF HE HAS NO MONEY, A YOUNG MAN WITH INITIATIVE COULD JUST PICK UP THAT MOUSE AND START A BUSINESS.

A DEAD MOUSE AS CAPITAL? HA! HA! HA!

THE YOUNG MAN STOPPED AND GAZED AT THE DEAD MOUSE.

IT SOUNDS LIKE AN ABSURD IDEA...

... BUT THE TREASURER MUST SURELY KNOW WHAT HE IS TALKING ABOUT!

BUT WHAT CAN I DO WITH IT?

WHO WOULD WANT TO BUY A DEAD MOUSE?

HEY, PUSSY, COME BACK!

AH! NOW I KNOW WHAT HAS ATTRACTED HIM!

MY FRIEND, WILL YOU SELL YOUR MOUSE TO ME? I'LL PAY ONE PAISA FOR IT.

THE MOUSE IS YOURS!

THE FIRST COIN I'VE EARNED!

BUT WHAT CAN I DO WITH THIS SMALL COIN? THE TREASURER HAD SAID ONE MUST HAVE ENTERPRISE... HMM.

OH! I'VE GOT IT. I MUST FIND OUT IF THERE IS A DEMAND FOR SOMETHING AND THEN ARRANGE TO SUPPLY IT!

PLEASE GIVE ME ONE PAISA'S WORTH OF GUR.

THE NEXT MORNING, THE YOUNG MAN FILLED A POT WITH DRINKING WATER AND WENT TO THE OUTSKIRTS OF THE CITY.

I'LL WAIT HERE FOR THE FLOWER-GATHERERS TO RETURN FROM WORK.

IN THE FOREST, WORKERS WERE BUSY COLLECTING FLOWERS.

IT WAS LATE IN THE AFTERNOON WHEN THEY FINISHED THEIR WORK AND BEGAN RETURNING TO THE CITY.

IT'S SO HOT! AND I'M SO THIRSTY!

THERE WON'T BE ANY WATER TO DRINK TILL WE REACH THE CITY.

AH! HERE THEY COME!

BROTHER, YOU MUST BE TIRED. HAVE SOME WATER AND A LITTLE GUR.

THANK YOU, SON. MAY YOU LIVE LONG.

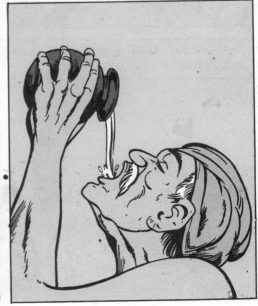

THERE HE SOLD THEM.

HERE IS THE MONEY.

IN A MINUTE, SIR.

A BUNCH FOR ME, TOO.

NOW I HAVE EIGHT COPPER PIECES.

WITH THE MONEY HE EARNED, THE YOUNG MAN BOUGHT A BIG WATER POT AND A LARGER QUANTITY OF GUR. THE NEXT DAY HE WENT BACK TO THE FOREST.

TODAY YOU MAY HAVE A LITTLE MORE GUR.

MAY GOD BLESS YOU, SON.

LATER, HE WENT EVEN FURTHER AWAY, TO THE FIELDS WHERE GRASS-CUTTERS WERE WORKING.

IS ANYBODY THIRSTY?

YOU WON'T FIND ANYONE HERE WHO IS NOT THIRSTY. GIVE ME SOME WATER, SON.

BROTHER, YOU ARE KIND TO US. WHAT CAN WE DO FOR YOU IN RETURN?

NOTHING AT PRESENT.

BUT DON'T HESITATE TO ASK US WHEN YOU NEED OUR HELP.

A MONTH PASSED BY. ONE EVENING, THE YOUNG MAN WAS RETURNING HOME, WHEN A STORM BROKE OUT.

EVERYWHERE, THE WIND BLEW DOWN LEAVES AND DRY BRANCHES.

IF THERE IS MONEY IN A DEAD MOUSE THERE SHOULD BE MONEY IN THESE LEAVES AND BRANCHES, TOO!

THE NEXT MORNING HE WENT TO THE PALACE GARDEN AND SPOKE TO THE GARDENER.

YOU LOOK WORRIED, UNCLE. CAN I HELP YOU?

HOW CAN YOU? THE GARDEN IS LITTERED WITH BRANCHES...

...AND THE KING IS EXPECTED ANY MOMENT NOW. I DON'T KNOW HOW TO CLEAR THE MESS BEFORE HE COMES.

I'LL HELP YOU IF I CAN KEEP THE FALLEN BRANCHES.

TAKE THEM, SON. ONLY, TAKE THEM AWAY SOON.

I'LL GO AND GET SOME HELP. I'LL BE BACK IN A MINUTE.

THE YOUNG MAN DID NOT HAVE TO GO FAR —

WOULD YOU LIKE TO HAVE SOME GUR?

GUR! OH, CERTAINLY!

9

THEN COME ON, BOYS. I'LL GIVE YOU SOME.

GIVE ME SOME!

AND ME, TOO!

EVERYONE WILL GET HIS SHARE.

WOULD YOU LIKE TO HAVE SOME MORE?

YES!

BUT YOU MUST EARN IT.

WE ARE READY!

TELL US WHAT WE SHOULD DO!

THEN COME WITH ME.

YOU MUST COLLECT ALL THE FALLEN BRANCHES AND HEAP THEM OUTSIDE THE GARDEN.

THAT'S EASY!

QUICKLY THEY GATHERED UP THE FALLEN BRANCHES.

AND FORMED A LONG HUMAN CHAIN TO PASS THEM ON...

...TO A PLACE OUTSIDE THE GARDEN.

AH! YOU HAVE FINISHED! HERE IS YOUR REWARD— DELICIOUS GUR!

THANK YOU!

THANK YOU!

JUST AS THE YOUNG MAN WAS WONDERING WHAT HE SHOULD DO NEXT...

...A POTTER CAME BY AND STOPPED HIS CART.

IS THAT FOR SALE?

YES!

HERE ARE SIXTEEN COPPER PIECES. PLEASE HELP ME LOAD MY CART.

YES, OF COURSE!

NOW I HAVE ALL THE WOOD I NEED TO FIRE THE POTS SPECIALLY ORDERED BY THE KING.

THE YOUNG MAN THEN WENT WITH THE POTTER...

... TO THE MARKET.

HAVE YOU HEARD? THE HORSE-DEALER WILL BE COMING TOMORROW.

YES, YES. I HEAR HE WILL BE BRINGING FIVE HUNDRED HORSES TO SELL.

AH, HA! THAT'S USEFUL INFORMATION! THANKS FOR LETTING ME KNOW!

HURRIEDLY, HE WENT TO THE GRASS-CUTTERS.

FRIENDS, I SEEK A FAVOUR OF YOU.

AT LAST! TELL US WHAT WE SHOULD DO.

I WANT A BUNDLE OF GRASS FROM EACH OF YOU.

WE ARE FIVE HUNDRED IN ALL — SO AS MANY BUNDLES OF GRASS WILL BE DELIVERED TO YOU TONIGHT.

AND I WANT YOU TO PROMISE THAT TILL TOMORROW AFTERNOON YOU WILL NOT SELL ANYONE ANY GRASS AT ALL.

YOU ARE OUR FRIEND. AND WE WILL DO WHAT YOU ASK WITHOUT QUESTION.

LATE THAT EVENING —

YOU SEE, WE HAVE KEPT OUR WORD!

I SHALL BE FOREVER INDEBTED TO YOU.

THE NEXT MORNING THE HORSE-DEALER ARRIVED WITH FIVE HUNDRED HORSES AT THE OUTSKIRTS OF VARANASI.

STRANGE! NO ONE HAS COME YET TO SELL ME GRASS FOR MY HORSES.

HE WENT TO THE MARKET.

NO GRASS IN VARANASI?

WHERE HAVE THE GRASS-CUTTERS GONE? I'D BETTER GO FURTHER— NEARER THE FIELDS.

GRASS! AT LAST!

14

A DAY LATER —

WHY IS IT SO QUIET HERE TODAY? IS ANYTHING THE MATTER?

EVERYONE IS AWAY MAKING PREPARATIONS TO RECEIVE THE BOATS THAT WILL BE ARRIVING TOMORROW.

BOATS... ARRIVING TOMORROW?

AN IDEA STRUCK HIM LIKE LIGHTNING —

HE BOUGHT NEW CLOTHES AND THEN WENT TO HIRE A CARRIAGE.

SEND THE CARRIAGE TO ME EARLY TOMORROW MORNING. HERE IS SOME MONEY AS AN ADVANCE.

VERY EARLY THE NEXT MORNING THE YOUNG MAN RODE IN STYLE TO THE RIVER HARBOUR WITH TWO FRIENDS...

...AND WAITED TO RECEIVE THE VISITING MERCHANT.

HE WAS, NATURALLY, THE FIRST TO GREET THE MERCHANT.

WELCOME TO VARANASI!

I AM HAPPY TO MEET YOU, SIR.

I WANT TO BUY ALL THE MERCHANDISE YOU HAVE BROUGHT.

RIGHT. IT IS A PLEASURE TO DO BUSINESS WITH YOU.

THE MERCHANT QUOTED A PRICE TO WHICH THE YOUNG MAN READILY AGREED.

I NEED TIME TO ARRANGE THE PAYMENT. MEANWHILE, HERE IS MY SIGNET RING AS SECURITY.

THEN THE YOUNG MAN SET UP A CANVAS SHELTER AND WAITED —

WHEN THE CITY MERCHANTS COME, BRING THEM IN WITH DUE COURTESY.

AT DAYBREAK, A HUNDRED MERCHANTS CAME TO THE HARBOUR.

MY FRIEND, WE HAVE COME TO DO BUSINESS WITH YOU!

I'M SORRY, SIR. I HAVE ALREADY SOLD EVERY-THING.

SOLD EVERYTHING! WHEN? TO WHOM?

TO THAT YOUNG MERCHANT OVER THERE.

HE IS NOT ONE OF US!

WE CAN'T LET ANY NEW PERSONS INTO OUR TRADE — OR WE'LL BE RUINED!

18

THAT WILL MAKE IT A HUNDRED THOUSAND PIECES SINCE THERE ARE A HUNDRED MERCHANTS HERE!

... MOREOVER, WE'D LIKE TO BUY YOUR SHARE IN IT TOO.

NO! NO!

BUT WE'LL PAY HANDSOMELY — ONE THOUSAND PIECES EACH.

THAT WILL MAKE IT ANOTHER HUNDRED THOUSAND GOLD PIECES!

HAVING AGREED TO THE DEAL, THE YOUNG MAN RETURNED HOME —

I WILL STILL HAVE A BIG AMOUNT LEFT AFTER PAYING THE MERCHANT. AND I OWE IT ALL TO THE TREASURER'S WISDOM!

TO SHOW HIS GRATITUDE, HE WENT TO CALL ON THE TREASURER, TAKING HALF HIS PROFITS WITH HIM.

SIR, PERMIT ME TO PRESENT YOU WITH THESE COINS AS MY HUMBLE GURU-DAKSHINA.

GURU-DAKSHINA!

BUT I HAVEN'T SEEN YOU BEFORE! I HAVEN'T TAUGHT YOU ANYTHING!

YES, YOU HAVE! I CAME BY ALL MY WEALTH IN FOUR SHORT MONTHS, SIMPLY BY FOLLOWING YOUR TEACHING.

THEN HE TOLD THE TREASURER THE WHOLE STORY, STARTING WITH THE DEAD MOUSE —

THIS YOUNG MAN IS EXTRAORDINARILY CLEVER —JUST THE PERSON I'D CHOOSE FOR MY LOVELY DAUGHTER.

SO HE MARRIED THE YOUNG MAN TO HIS DAUGHTER AND GAVE HIM ALL HIS FAMILY ESTATES.

THE GODDESS OF SUCCESS SMILES ON THOSE WHO SHOW INITIATIVE. MAY YOU ALWAYS BE SO FORTUNATE, MY SON!

THE INVALUABLE TREASURE

IN VARANASI, THERE ONCE LIVED A WATER-CARRIER.

THOUGH HE WORKED HARD, HE BARELY EARNED ENOUGH FOR TWO MEALS A DAY.

HOWEVER, ONE DAY HE MADE A LITTLE EXTRA MONEY.

ONE PAISA!

BUT WHERE SHALL I HIDE MY TREASURE?

IT WILL BE SAFE BEHIND ONE OF THESE BRICKS.

22

HE BEGAN GENTLY TO TAP AT THE BRICKS.

AH! I THINK I'VE FOUND A LOOSE BRICK!

IT'S THE FIRST BRICK TO THE LEFT OF THE NORTHERN GATE...

...AND THE TENTH ONE FROM THE GROUND LEVEL.

THE PLACE WILL BE EASY TO REMEMBER.

THAT WAS THE ONLY TIME HE HAD EARNED A LITTLE MORE THAN HE ABSOLUTELY NEEDED. HE HAD NEVER HAD SUCH LUCK BEFORE.

AH! MY TREASURE IS SAFE THERE. I AM A RICH MAN!

THE YEARS PASSED BY. HE MARRIED A GIRL WHO ALSO WORKED AS A WATER-CARRIER. THEY BUILT A HUT NEAR THE SOUTHERN GATE OF THE CITY. ONE AFTERNOON —

I WISH WE COULD GO TO TOWN THIS EVENING TO ATTEND THE FAIR! BUT WE DON'T HAVE ENOUGH MONEY.

OF COURSE, WE DO! I HAVE MONEY — ONE PAISA! I'VE HIDDEN IT AWAY IN A SAFE PLACE.

I, TOO, HAVE ONE PAISA. IF YOU'LL BRING YOURS, WE'LL HAVE ENOUGH TO ENJOY OURSELVES.

I WILL GO NOW AND BRING YOU MY TREASURE.

COME BACK SOON!

YES, YES, I'LL BE BACK AT ONCE!

IT WAS SUMMER. THE MIDDAY SUN WAS BLAZING IN THE SKY. NO ONE WAS TO BE SEEN ON THE STREETS EXCEPT THE WATER-CARRIER WHO WAS RUNNING WITH A SONG ON HIS LIPS.

AH! THERE'S THE PLACE! ONLY A LITTLE MORE DISTANCE TO GO!

KING UDAYA, WHO WAS RELAXING IN THE PALACE BALCONY, SAW THE WATER-CARRIER.

I WONDER WHAT MAKES HIM RUN AT THIS TIME OF THE DAY, LOOKING SO HAPPY!

HE SENT WORD TO HAVE THE MAN BROUGHT TO HIM —

HEY! STOP!

LET ME GO!

THE KING WANTS TO SPEAK TO YOU. COME!

I HAVE MORE IMPORTANT THINGS TO DO. I HAVE NO TIME TO MEET THE KING ....

WHAT A SIMPLE MAN! DON'T YOU REALISE IT IS AN HONOUR TO BE TAKEN BEFORE THE KING?

THE GUARDS HAD TO USE FORCE TO TAKE THE WATER-CARRIER TO THE KING.

26

THE KING ASKED IF IT WERE A THOUSAND, A HUNDRED, FIFTY, TEN GOLD COINS. BUT THE WATER-CARRIER SHOOK HIS HEAD —

NO, NO. NOT THAT MUCH!

THEN HOW MUCH IS IT?

IT IS ONE PAISA, MY KING.

ONE PAISA!

YES, WITH THAT MONEY I CAN BUY A LOT OF THINGS FOR MY WIFE AND MAKE HER HAPPY.

MY FRIEND, YOU DON'T HAVE TO RUN TO THE NORTHERN GATE TO GET ONE PAISA. I WILL GIVE IT TO YOU.

HERE, TAKE THIS AND GO HOME.

I WILL TAKE WHAT YOU GIVE ME. BUT I WILL GO AND GET THE OTHER COIN, TOO.

MY FRIEND, DON'T EXERT YOURSELF. I WILL GIVE YOU TWO PAISAS.

I WILL ACCEPT THEM. ALL THE SAME, I WILL GET THE OTHER ONE, TOO.

I WILL GIVE YOU TEN. PLEASE RETURN HOME.

I'LL TAKE TEN—BUT THE OTHER ONE, TOO.

HE IS SO ATTACHED TO THE ONE PAISA HE HAS SAVED! BUT POOR MAN! HE'LL HAVE TO RUN ALL THE WAY TO THE NORTHERN GATE TO GET IT!

THE KING RAISED HIS OFFER.

I WILL GIVE YOU A HUNDRED PAISAS.

A THOUSAND!

TEN THOUSAND!

THANK YOU. I WILL TAKE ALL YOU OFFER— AND THE ONE I HAVE HIDDEN, TOO.

IS THERE NO WAY I CAN SAVE HIM FROM THIS STUBBORNNESS?

DESPERATELY, THE KING RAISED HIS OFFER AGAIN AND AGAIN. BUT THE WATER-CARRIER INSISTED THAT HE WOULD GO AND FETCH HIS HIDDEN TREASURE. FINALLY —

I WILL GIVE YOU HALF MY KINGDOM IF ONLY YOU WILL AGREE TO DROP THE IDEA OF RUNNING NOW FOR ONE PAISA!

I AGREE!

AT LAST! I AM HAPPY TO HAVE YOUR AGREEMENT!

THE KING HELD A DARBAR TO CROWN THE WATER-CARRIER KING OF ONE HALF OF THE KINGDOM.

NOW, FRIEND, TELL ME WHICH HALF OF THE KINGDOM YOU CHOOSE TO HAVE.

THE WATER-CARRIER THOUGHT FOR A SECOND —

I WANT THE NORTHERN HALF OF THE KINGDOM.

YOU'VE WON AGAIN!

THUS, THE WATER-CARRIER NOT ONLY GOT HALF THE KINGDOM BUT ALSO HIS TREASURE WHICH WAS HIDDEN IN THE NORTHERN WALL.

THE RIGHT MOMENT

KING SUVARNAKA WAS A GENEROUS MONARCH. NO SUPPLICANT EVER LEFT WITHOUT RECEIVING A GIFT FROM HIM...

...EXCEPT YASHOVARMAN.

I DO WISH TO GIVE YOU GIFTS. BUT THE SUN GOD PREVENTS ME FROM DOING SO.

AS LONG AS HE IS WATCHING, I CANNOT GRATIFY YOUR WISH.

ONLY TWO CATEGORIES OF PEOPLE DESERVE GIFTS — THE OLD AND INFIRM OR THE PANDITS.

HE IS NOT INFIRM. SO LET ME SEE IF HE HAS HIS WITS ABOUT HIM.

31

EACH DAY THE KING WOULD POINT AT THE SUN AND YASHOVARMAN WOULD LEAVE DISAPPOINTED.

BUT ONE DAY —.

MAHARAJ, I HAVE BEEN SEEKING ALMS OF YOU FOR A LONG TIME NOW.

I KNOW. BUT THE SUN GOD...

AS THE KING LOOKED UP HE DID NOT SEE THE SUN.

OH!

THERE WAS A TOTAL SOLAR ECLIPSE.

WHATEVER YOU WISH TO GIVE PLEASE GIVE NOW...

...WHEN MY ENEMY IS STILL IN THE GRIP OF HIS ENEMY*.

HA! HA!

THE KING REMOVED HIS GOLD NECKLACE AND YASHOVARMAN RECEIVED HIS GIFT AT LAST.

GLORY BE TO YOU, MAHARAJ.

* ACCORDING TO PURANAS AN ECLIPSE IS CAUSED WHEN THE SUN OR THE MOON IS SWALLOWED BY THE DEMONS RAHU OR KETU.

THE MAGIC CHANT

A PANDIT AND HIS PUPIL WERE ONCE PASSING THROUGH A FOREST.

SUDDENLY —

HALT! WHO GOES THERE?

ROBBERS!

WE HAVE NO MONEY. PLEASE LET US GO.

HA! HA! YOU CANNOT DECEIVE US WITH HUMBLE TALK AND SIMPLE CLOTHES! IF YOU ARE CARRYING NO MONEY, YOUR PUPIL CAN BRING IT FROM YOUR HOUSE.

THEY BOUND THE PANDIT TO A TREE.

RUN FAST AND BRING A THOUSAND GOLD COINS. ONLY THEN WILL YOUR GURU BE FREED!

MASTER, I'LL COME BACK AS SOON AS POSSIBLE. SO PLEASE DO NOT TELL THESE THUGS THAT YOU KNOW THE VAIDARBHA MANTRA!

THE VAIDARBHA MANTRA IS A CHANT KNOWN TO VERY FEW. IF UTTERED WHEN THE STARS ARE IN A FAVOURABLE POSITION, IT PRODUCES A SHOWER OF GEMS.

NOW HURRY UP, BOY, AND DO WHAT YOU'VE BEEN TOLD!

I'LL COME BACK WITH THE MONEY IN TWO DAYS.

THAT NIGHT —

HOW COLD IT IS! ALL MY JOINTS ACHE! I WISH I COULD WARM MYSELF NEAR THAT FIRE. BUT THEY WILL KEEP ME TIED TO THIS TREE TILL MY PUPIL RETURNS!

THE PANDIT LOOKED UP AT THE SKY —

OH! THE PLANETS ARE MOVING INTO THE CORRECT POSITION. SHOULD I TELL THE ROBBERS ABOUT THE VAIDARBHA MANTRA AND SO BE FREE AGAIN?

REMEMBERING HIS PUPIL'S ADVICE, HE HESITATED. BUT FINALLY —

AFTER ALL, WHAT IS THE USE OF KNOWLEDGE IF ONE CANNOT UTILISE IT IN TIMES OF CRISIS?

HEY, CHIEF! LISTEN! I HAVE SOMETHING IMPORTANT TO SAY!

IF I START A SHOWER OF GEMS, WILL YOU LET ME GO?

A SHOWER OF GEMS? ARE YOU JOKING?

NO, I'M SERIOUS. I CAN DO IT BY MEANS OF A MAGIC CHANT.

BUT...!

IN A FEW MOMENTS THE PLANETS WILL BE IN THE RIGHT POSITION. THEN I CAN BEGIN.

ALL RIGHT, GO AHEAD!

I CAN'T DO IT WITHOUT HAVING A RITUAL BATH AND CHANGING INTO CLEAN SILK CLOTHES...

...AND, OF COURSE, YOU WILL FIRST HAVE TO SET ME FREE!

ALL RIGHT. BUT DON'T PLAY ANY TRICKS OR IT WILL BE THE WORSE FOR YOU!

SO THE PANDIT WAS SET FREE, AND AFTER A DIP IN THE RIVER, HE SAT FOR A LONG TIME, RECITING THE CHANT.

CAN HE REALLY DO IT, OR IS HE FOOLING US?

WILL IT HAPPEN?

HOW LONG WILL IT TAKE?

FINALLY, HE FINISHED.

THE VERY NEXT MOMENT —

GEMS! THOSE ARE PRECIOUS GEMS FALLING DOWN!

4

OF WHAT USE COULD THAT KNOCK-KNEED PANDIT BE TO ME?

HE'S INVALUABLE! HE KNOWS A MAGIC CHANT THAT WILL BRING DOWN A SHOWER OF JEWELS. THAT'S HOW WE CAME BY OURS!

OH, IN THAT CASE, WE WILL SET YOU FREE AND KEEP ONLY THE PANDIT!

THE CHIEF OF THE SECOND GANG TURNED TO THE PANDIT.

MY FRIEND, LET'S HAVE A BIG SHOWER OF GEMS!

YOU SHALL HAVE IT — BUT ONLY AFTER ONE YEAR.

DON'T MAKE A FOOL OF ME. I WANT THE JEWELS NOW!

I...I'M...SORRY. THE CHANT IS EFFECTIVE ONLY AT A SPECIFIC TIME. THE AUSPICIOUS MOMENT WILL NOT OCCUR AGAIN FOR ANOTHER YEAR.

LIAR! SCOUNDREL! WE WON'T LET YOU GET AWAY WITH IT.

7

A FIERCE FIGHT ENSUED...

... AND THE FIRST GANG WAS VANQUISHED —

NOW THE GEMS ARE MINE!

NO, MINE!

MINE!

YOU RASCAL, TAKE THAT!

SUDDENLY —

CHIEF! LOOK! HE IS RIDING AWAY WITH THE GEMS!

HEY! YOU! STOP!

'I'LL HIDE BEHIND THIS ROCK AND SURPRISE HIM WHEN HE COMES BACK.

MEANWHILE, THE OTHER ROBBER WENT TO THE VILLAGE NEAR BY AND BOUGHT SOME FOOD. ON HIS WAY BACK —

I'M STARVING. I'LL EAT FIRST AND THEN TAKE THE REST FOR MY FRIEND.

BUT, REALLY, HE IS NO FRIEND OF MINE AT ALL. WHY SHOULD I SHARE ANYTHING WITH HIM?

I WILL SHARE NEITHER FOOD NOR JEWELS WITH HIM. I'LL GET RID OF HIM!

SO HE SPRINKLED SOME POISON ON THE REMAINING FOOD.

THEN HE SET OFF AGAIN.

THIS WILL TAKE CARE OF HIM!

10

BUT WHEN HE ARRIVED —

THE TREASURE IS ALL MINE NOW!

AAH!

AND NOW, FOR SOME FOOD. AH! I AM AS RICH AS A KING TODAY!

BUT IT WAS ALL IN VAIN. FOR, HAVING EATEN THE POISONED FOOD, HE, TOO, FELL DEAD.

WHEN, TWO DAYS LATER, THE PUPIL RETURNED WITH THE MONEY, HE FOUND THE PLACE LITTERED WITH CORPSES.

MY GURU USED THE CHANT FOR THE BENEFIT OF UNDESERVING PEOPLE! IF ONLY HE HAD HEEDED MY ADVICE!

THE DRUMMER

A DRUMMER AND HIS SON ONCE WENT TO VARANASI TO PLAY AT A FESTIVAL.

AT THE END OF THE FESTIVAL —

HERE IS SOME MONEY FOR BOTH OF YOU. YOUR SON IS A VERY GOOD DRUMMER.

AND HERE ARE SOME JEWELS.

AND SOME CLOTHES.

FATHER, I ENJOYED THE FESTIVAL VERY MUCH.

YOU GAVE A GOOD PERFORMANCE, SON.

THE NEXT MOMENT —

WHAT ARE YOU DOING?

BEATING THE DRUM — WHAT ELSE? I FEEL ON TOP OF THE WORLD TODAY, FATHER!

DON'T MAKE SUCH A DIN! YOU WILL ATTRACT ROBBERS! THIS FOREST IS FULL OF THEM!

I'LL PLAY A MARTIAL BEAT TO FRIGHTEN THEM OFF, FATHER!

SOME THIEVES HIDING IN THE JUNGLE HEARD THE LOUD DRUMMING.

IT APPEARS A ROYAL PARTY IS HUNTING IN THE FOREST.

AFTER A WHILE —

ENOUGH, SON! DON'T DO IT AGAIN! THAT SHOULD ONLY BE PLAYED ONCE!

BUT THE BOY WENT ON —

STOP! WHY DON'T YOU LISTEN TO ME?

OH, FATHER, YOU WORRY TOO MUCH! I'LL SCARE THE THIEVES GOOD AND PROPER!

WHAT! THE SAME DRUM-BEATS THRICE! THAT IS NO ROYAL PARTY.

IT IS JUST SOMEBODY WHO HAS MADE A LOT OF MONEY AND IS FEELING HAPPY!

LET'S ATTACK HIM!

THE THIEVES QUICKLY SPOTTED THE DRUMMER AND HIS SON.

OH, YES! THOSE TWO CERTAINLY HAVE SOME MONEY IN THOSE HEAVY BUNDLES!

STOP! DON'T MOVE!

GIVE US ALL YOU HAVE!

WHAT A LOVELY NECKLACE!

THE CLOTHES ARE NEW, TOO.

AND THE THIEVES RAN OFF WITH THE LOOT.

I TOLD YOU TO STOP, DIDN'T I? BUT YOU WOULDN'T LISTEN. IN YOUR PRIDE, YOU FOOLISHLY INVITED YOUR OWN DOOM BY PLAYING AT THE WRONG TIME!

I HAVE LEARNT MY LESSON NOW, FATHER!

THE SADHU AND THE RAM

ONE DAY, THERE WAS GREAT EXCITEMENT IN VARANASI. PEOPLE HAD GATHERED TO WATCH A RAM-FIGHT.

A SADHU HAPPENED TO PASS BY.

WHAT IS GOING ON?

A RAM-FIGHT! OH, WHAT FINE BEASTS THEY ARE!

THE SADHU PUSHED HIS WAY IN.

HE SAW A RAM RETREATING WITH HIS HEAD BOWED LOW.

HE IS STEPPING BACK! HE IS BOWING BEFORE ME!

O, NOBLE BEAST! ONLY YOU, IN THIS WHOLE CROWD OF PEOPLE, KNOW A GREAT SOUL WHEN YOU SEE ONE!

A MAN IN THE CROWD CALLED OUT IN WARNING —

BE CAREFUL! HE IS NOT BOWING BEFORE YOU...!

...HE IS PREPARING TO ATTACK! PLEASE STEP BACK!

NO, I WON'T! THE POOR ANIMAL WANTS ME TO BLESS HIM!

A MOMENT LATER —

A-A-H!

I HAVE INVITED THIS AGONY ON MYSELF! I WAS FOOLISH AND VAIN! NOW I HAVE PAID THE PRICE!

THE DAY THE EARTH BROKE INTO TWO

ONE DAY A RABBIT WAS RELAXING UNDER A BILVA TREE ...

...WHEN A STRANGE THOUGHT STRUCK HIM —

I WONDER WHAT WILL HAPPEN IF THE EARTH BREAKS INTO TWO?

JUST THEN, A BILVA FRUIT FELL FROM THE TREE...

THUD

WH... WHAT IS THAT?

...AND ROLLED OVER DRY PALM LEAVES.

IS THE EARTH REALLY GOING TO BREAK? I MUST RUN AWAY TO A SAFE PLACE!

VERY SOON A PANIC-STRICKEN TROUPE WAS FLEEING THROUGH THE FOREST.

THEN A LION CAME BY ——

WHAT'S GOING ON HERE?

OH, DON'T YOU KNOW? THE EARTH IS BREAKING!

HMM.... BUT THAT IS IMPOSSIBLE!

HE CLIMBED TO THE TOP OF A HILL AND ROARED.

GR-GR-GR-GR

THE ANIMALS FROZE IN THEIR TRACKS.

WHY ARE YOU RUNNING? WHAT IS THE MATTER?

THE EARTH IS BREAKING, O MIGHTY ONE!

WE MUST GO AWAY FROM HERE!

WHO SAW THIS HAPPEN?

THE ELEPHANT. ASK HIM!

NO, NO. NOT ME. ASK THE TIGER.

OH, NO! THE PANTHER REPORTED IT TO ME. ASK HIM!

FINALLY, THE RABBIT WAS BROUGHT TO THE LION.

DID YOU REALLY SEE THE EARTH BREAKING, LITTLE ONE?

YES, MY LORD. I SAW IT WITH MY OWN EYES.

TELL ME, WHERE WAS THIS?

IT WAS NEAR MY BURROW WHICH IS UNDER A BILVA TREE IN A PALM GROVE.

I WAS JUST LYING DOWN THERE WONDERING WHAT I WOULD DO IF THE EARTH WERE TO BREAK, WHEN SUDDENLY...

... IT HAPPENED! I HEARD A DEAFENING NOISE AND FLED.

A PALM GROVE... A BILVA TREE... HMM.... I AM SURE HE HAS MADE A MISTAKE.

I'LL GO WITH THE RABBIT AND FIND OUT WHAT REALLY HAPPENED. WAIT HERE TILL I COME BACK.

VERY WELL, O MIGHTY ONE!

AND THE LION WENT OFF WITH THE RABBIT.

WHEN THEY REACHED THE PALM GROVE —

SHOW ME THE PLACE WHERE YOU HEARD THE NOISE. DON'T BE AFRAID. I'M HERE TO PROTECT YOU.

THAT'S THE BILVA TREE WHERE I HEARD THE THUNDERING NOISE!

ALL RIGHT. YOU WAIT FOR ME HERE. I'LL GO AND LOOK AROUND.

THE LION LOOKED CLOSELY AT THE PALM LEAVES UNDERNEATH THE BILVA TREE.

AH! JUST AS I THOUGHT! THE SOUND OF THE FRUIT FALLING ON DRY LEAVES FRIGHTENED THE RABBIT AND HE THOUGHT THAT THE EARTH WAS BREAKING.

RETURNING TO THE WAITING ANIMALS, THE LION TOLD THEM WHAT HE HAD DISCOVERED.

FRIENDS, YOU DID NOT CHECK IF THIS WAS TRUE. BLINDLY RELYING ON A FALSE RUMOUR, YOU WOULD HAVE PAID A HEAVY PRICE TODAY.

THE FOOLISH TREE

LONG AGO, TWO TREES LIVED IN PEACE AND FRIENDSHIP IN A FOREST WHICH WAS FULL OF WILD BEASTS.

LIONS AND TIGERS ROAMED FREELY IN THE FOREST AND PREYED ON OTHER ANIMALS.

AFTER THEY HAD HAD THEIR FILL, THEY LEFT THE CARCASSES BEHIND...

...CAUSING A FOUL STENCH ALL ROUND. THE FOREST WAS REEKING WITH THE SMELL. ONE DAY —

FRIEND, THESE ANIMALS ARE SUCH A NUISANCE! I FEEL SUFFOCATED BY THE SMELL.

YES, IT IS BECOMING DIFFICULT TO LIVE HERE.

I CAN'T BEAR IT ANY LONGER! I'LL DRIVE THESE ANIMALS AWAY.

OH, NO! PLEASE DON'T! THE WILD ANIMALS PROTECT US, AND KEEP MEN AWAY!

BUT JUST IMAGINE, HOW PURE AND PLEASANT THE AIR WILL BE!

I'LL DO IT! I'LL DRIVE THEM AWAY!

OH, MY FRIEND! YOU DON'T KNOW WHAT YOU ARE DOING!

ONE NIGHT, SHORTLY AFTERWARDS —

AH! A STRONG BREEZE IS BLOWING THIS WAY. HERE IS MY CHANCE!

THE TREE SHOOK ITSELF VIGOROUSLY, MAKING A LOUD NOISE...

SHR-SHR-SHR!

...WHICH AWAKENED THE ANIMALS SLEEPING BENEATH IT.

WHAT'S HAPPENING?

LOOK AT THAT TREE!

HOW IT IS SWAYING!

THE TREE IS POSSESSED!

LET'S RUN AWAY!

YES, ALL OF US HAD BETTER LEAVE!

HURRY!

THE NEXT MORNING —

AT LAST, I'VE GOT RID OF THOSE ANIMALS! ALREADY, THE AIR SMELLS FRESHER!

MANY DAYS PASSED. QUIET AND PEACE REIGNED IN THE FOREST. THEN ONE AFTERNOON, A COWHERD PASSED THAT WAY.

SH...O...O... COME BACK, YOU NAUGHTY ONE! THE LION WILL EAT YOU UP!

FOLLOWING THE CALF, THE BOY VENTURED INTO THE FOREST.

I HOPE A TIGER DOESN'T POUNCE ON ME!

BUT THERE SEEM TO BE NO TIGERS HERE! AND NO ANIMAL FOOTPRINTS ANYWHERE AROUND!

HE WENT HOME AND TOLD HIS FAMILY ABOUT THIS DISCOVERY. THE NEXT DAY —

IT LOOKS AS IF NO ANIMALS HAVE LIVED HERE FOR AGES!

HE IS RIGHT!

THIS LAND COULD BE VERY USEFUL TO US.

YOU SEE WHAT THEY ARE PLANNING? I HAD TOLD YOU TO LET THE WILD BEASTS ALONE.

DON'T BE SILLY. I CAN FRIGHTEN THOSE MEN AWAY, AS I DID THE BEASTS!

THE TREE SHOOK ITSELF VIOLENTLY, MAKING A LOUD SOUND —

SHR...SHR...SH

WHAT IS THAT AWFUL SOUND, FATHER?

IT'S NOTHING, SON! JUST THE BREEZE, RUSTLING THROUGH THE LEAVES!

THE TREE TRIED AGAIN.

SHR...SHI

HEY! WATCH OUT!

OH! IT'S NOTHING TO WORRY ABOUT! JUST A FEW TWIGS HAVE FALLEN DOWN! WE'LL CUT DOWN THESE TREES. THE WOOD WILL COME IN USEFUL.

SOON THE FOREST WAS FULL OF PEOPLE FROM THE VILLAGE NEAR BY.

JUST A FEW MORE STROKES, BROTHER!

YES, THEN THE TREE WILL FALL DOWN.

WE'LL TACKLE THIS TREE TOMORROW.

THEY'RE POINTING TO ME! WHAT SHALL I DO?

THAT NIGHT —

HELP, FRIEND! HELP ME, PLEASE! YOU HEARD THEM, DIDN'T YOU? THEY ARE COMING FOR ME TOMORROW!

IT IS TOO LATE! NOW YOU MUST BEAR THE CONSEQUENCES OF YOUR ACTION!

AND THAT WAS THE END OF THE TREE.

THE LOST GRAM

ONCE A KING AND HIS ARMY HAD ENCAMPED OUTSIDE A CITY.

A MONKEY WATCHED THEM CLOSELY FROM A TREE.

I HAVE BEEN FEELING HUNGRY ALL DAY BUT NOW IT APPEARS I'LL HAVE A FEAST!

A LITTLE LATER —

LET'S ROAST SOME GRAM FOR THE HORSES.

HA! JUST AS I EXPECTED. HOW LUCKY I AM!

WE'LL FEED THE HORSES WHEN THE GRAM GETS COLD.

THIS IS MY CHANCE!

AS THE SOLDIERS TURNED TO LEAVE, THE MONKEY SWOOPED DOWN FROM THE TREE...

... AND ATE A HANDFUL OF GRAM.

THIS IS DELICIOUS!

BUT THOUGH HIS HUNGER WAS SATISFIED, HIS GREED WAS NOT.

I MUST TAKE AWAY AS MUCH AS I CAN!

HE STUFFED HIS MOUTH WITH GRAM...

... AND GRABBED SOME MORE WITH BOTH FRONT PAWS.

I'LL HAVE ENOUGH FOR MANY MORE DAYS!

HA! NOW I'LL EAT SOME MORE!

BUT ONE GRAIN ROLLED OUT AND...

...FELL ON THE GROUND.

OH... OH, MY GRAM! IT'S GONE!

The Priceless Gem

AUSHADHA KUMAR WAS A REINCARNATION OF THE BODHISATTVA.

HE WAS NAMED AUSHADHA* KUMAR, BECAUSE HE WAS BORN HOLDING A DIVINE HERB WHICH HAD SUPERNATURAL HEALING POWERS.

A YEAR BEFORE AUSHADHA KUMAR'S BIRTH, KING VAIDEHA OF MITHILA HAD A DREAM SIGNIFYING THE ADVENT OF A GREAT SOUL WHOSE WISDOM WOULD BE UNSURPASSED.

EIGHT YEARS LATER, CONVINCED THAT AUSHADHA WAS THAT GREAT SOUL, KING VAIDEHA ADOPTED HIM AND BROUGHT HIM TO MITHILA.

AT MITHILA, WHILE AUSHADHA GREW UP INTO A HANDSOME YOUNGSTER, THE PANDITS OF THE COURT, WHO NEVER WANTED HIM THERE IN THE FIRST PLACE BECAME ENVIOUS OF HIM.

* MEDICINE

AFTER SEVERAL ATTEMPTS —

NO, I CAN'T REACH IT.

THEN LET US INFORM THE KING.

WHEN VAIDEHA ARRIVED AT THE TANK—

THERE IT IS, MAHARAJ.

YES, I SEE IT.

NO MAN CAN GET TO IT. MY FRIEND IS THE BEST SWIMMER IN THE LAND BUT...

...EVEN HE COULD NOT.

THAT FABULOUS GEM MUST BE RECOVERED.

SENAKA, A COURT PANDIT AND THE CHIEF COUNSELLOR, OBSERVED THAT VAIDEHA'S HEART WAS SET ON THE GEM.

IF I RETRIEVE IT, THE KING WILL HAVE GREATER FAITH IN ME THAN HE HAS IN AUSHADHA KUMAR.

SO BEFORE VAIDEHA COULD APPROACH AUSHADHA KUMAR —

I SHALL RECOVER THE GEM RIGHT AWAY, MAHARAJ.

ALL RIGHT, SENAKA.

COME ON MEN, DRAIN THE TANK.

WAIT! THAT IS NOT THE...

PLEASE DO NOT INTERFERE. THE TASK HAS BEEN ASSIGNED TO ME.

4

WHAT! THE GEM HAS VANISHED!

HM...M...MPH! THEN HAVE THE TANK REPAIRED AND REFILLED.

SOON THE TANK WAS FILLED AGAIN WITH WATER AND LO! THERE WAS THE GEM, GLITTERING AWAY AS BEFORE.

HOW DID IT GET THERE, SENAKA?

THE GEM IS NOT IN THE TANK.

THEN HOW IS IT SEEN THERE?

BRING ME A THALI* AND I WILL SHOW YOU HOW.

A THALI WAS BROUGHT. AUSHADHA FILLED IT WITH WATER AND HELD IT OUT.

MAHARAJ, THE GEM YOU SEE IN THIS THALI...

...IS ONLY A REFLECTION. THE REAL GEM IS IN THE CROW'S NEST IN THAT PALM TREE.

* BRASS PLATE

6

CAW, CAW.

AUSHADHA KUMAR PRESENTED THE PRICE- LESS GEM TO THE KING.

WELL DONE, AUSHADHA!

AROUND THIS TIME A YOUNG MAN NAMED PINGUTTAR, WHO HAD COMPLETED HIS STUDIES, WAS TAKING LEAVE OF HIS TEACHER WHEN —

WAIT, SON! TRADITION DEMANDS THAT YOU, MY SENIOR- MOST DISCIPLE, SHOULD WED MY ELIGIBLE DAUGHTER.

BUT SIR... I... ER...

YOUNG MAN, TRADITION MAKES US WHAT WE ARE.

WE MUST OBEY THE DICTATES OF TRADITION AT ALL COSTS.

SHE IS SO BEAUTIFUL AND I AM SO HOMELY.

AND SHE IS FAR MORE INTELLIGENT THAN I AM.

I SHALL ALWAYS FEEL INFERIOR TO HER. I MUST GET RID OF HER SOMEHOW.

SOON, THEY CAME UPON A GOOLAR* TREE IN THE JUNGLE. PINGUTTAR SUDDENLY FELT HUNGRY.

I WILL EAT SOME GOOLARS.

HE CLIMBED UP THE TREE AND STARTED GOBBLING THE FRUIT.

* WILD FIG.

PLEASE PLUCK SOME FOR ME TOO.

PLUCK THEM YOUR-SELF.

HIS POOR WIFE WAS FORCED TO CLIMB THE TREE.

THE MOMENT SHE CLIMBED UP, PINGUTTAR CAME DOWN...

...QUICKLY COLLECTED AS MANY THORNY TWIGS AS HE COULD...

...AND PLACED THEM AROUND THE TRUNK OF THE TREE.

WHAT ARE YOU DOING?

GETTING RID OF YOU. I DID NOT WANT TO MARRY YOU, YOUR FATHER FORCED YOU ON ME.

I AM OFF. IF YOU TRY TO COME DOWN, THE THORNS WILL PRICK YOU.

HIS HAPLESS WIFE WAS STRANDED IN THE TREE.

A FEW DAYS LATER —

WHAT IS THAT WOMAN DOING UP THERE ON THAT TREE?

I WILL FIND OUT, SIR.

WHEN THE WOMAN NARRATED HER STORY —

HE MUST HAVE BEEN OUT OF HIS MIND TO ABANDON SUCH AN EXCEPTIONAL BEAUTY.

WHAT SHALL WE DO ABOUT HER?

IT IS A KING'S DHARMA TO PROTECT THE UNPROTECTED.

HEEDING THE ADVICE OF HIS MINISTER, KING VAIDEHA BROUGHT HER TO HIS PALACE.

EVEN IN THE HOUR OF CRISIS SHE WAS SO CALM. SHE IS FIT TO BE A QUEEN.

THE WISE SAY THAT A WOMAN ABANDONED BY HER HUSBAND CAN REMARRY. WILL YOU MARRY ME?

GLADLY, O NOBLE KING!

AND ON AN AUSPICIOUS DAY, THE KING MARRIED HER.

YOU ARE NOW BEGINNING A NEW LIFE. SO I MUST GIVE YOU A NEW NAME.

SINCE I FOUND YOU ON AN UDUMBARA* TREE, I SHALL CALL YOU UDUMBARA DEVI.

✽ WILD FIG — GOOLAR

KING VAIDEHA AND QUEEN UDUMBARA DEVI LED A HAPPY LIFE FOR SOME TIME.

THEN, ONE DAY —

THAT MAN? HE LOOKS LIKE...

YES, IT IS HIM. WHAT A FATE!

AND THE QUEEN SUDDENLY SMILED. THE KING SAW HER SMILE AND BECAME ANGRY.

HOW DARE YOU SMILE AT A STRANGE MAN?

HE IS THE MAN WHO ABANDONED ME.

BEING A WOMAN OF NOBLE CHARACTER, SHE COULD NOT HAVE LEFT HER HUSBAND. AND...

...IF HER HUSBAND HAD NOT ABANDONED HER, SHE WOULD BE LEADING A MISERABLE LIFE TODAY.

SO, WHEN I SAW THE PLIGHT OF THE MAN, I COULD NOT HELP BEING PLEASED WITH MY FATE. THAT IS WHY I SMILED.

WHEN THE FACTS WERE VERIFIED, THE KING WAS SATISFIED.

THANK YOU, AUSHADHA. BUT FOR YOU I WOULD HAVE LOST A GEM AMONG WOMEN.

BY THEN, KING VAIDEHA HAD SENSED THAT SENAKA AND OTHER PANDITS WERE ENVIOUS OF AUSHADHA. TO PROVE AUSHADHA'S WISDOM, VAIDEHA POSED A RIDDLE TO THEM.

I WANT TO KNOW WHO IS SUPERIOR, A MAN WHO IS RICH BUT STUPID OR A MAN WHO IS WISE BUT POOR.

THE RICH ONE IS SUPERIOR WITHOUT DOUBT.

WHY?

BECAUSE THE POOR, HOWEVER KNOWLEDGE-ABLE, HAVE TO SERVE THE RICH.

AUSHADHA, WHAT DO YOU HAVE TO SAY?

MAHARAJ, I SAY THE WISE ONE IS FAR SUPERIOR.

WHY?

BECAUSE, THE STUPID SEE WEALTH AS AN END IN ITSELF AND HENCE COMMIT SINS, WHEREAS THE WISE DO NOT AND ARE HENCE VIRTUOUS.

BUT THE RICH HOWEVER STUPID LIVE WELL. THEY MAKE USE OF ALL...

...INCLUDING THE WISE WHO ARE POOR!

NOT FOR LONG. FOR THE RICH WHO ARE STUPID DO NOT HAVE THE SENSE TO EMPLOY WISE ADVISERS.

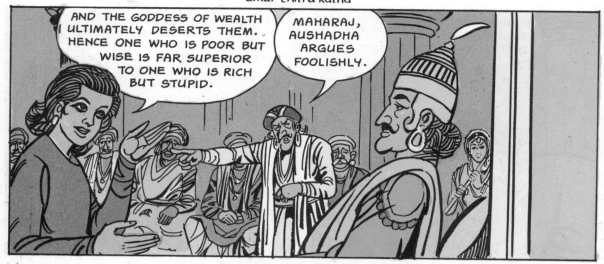

AND THE GODDESS OF WEALTH ULTIMATELY DESERTS THEM. HENCE ONE WHO IS POOR BUT WISE IS FAR SUPERIOR TO ONE WHO IS RICH BUT STUPID.

MAHARAJ, AUSHADHA ARGUES FOOLISHLY.

NOW LOOK AT US. DON'T WE, YOUR COUNSELLORS, THOUGH WE ARE PANDITS, BOW BEFORE YOU? DOES NOT THAT PROVE MY POINT?

ON THE CONTRARY!

KINGS CANNOT FUNCTION WITHOUT WISE COUNSELLORS. HENCE THE WISE ARE DEFINITELY SUPERIOR.

SENAKA COULD NOT REFUTE THAT.

YOUR LOGIC IS ASTOUNDING, AUSHADHA. YOU DESERVE SIXTEEN VILLAGES AS A REWARD.

I AM GRATEFUL, MAHARAJ.

QUEEN UDUMBARA DEVI WAS HAPPY WITH THE GROWING STATUS OF AUSHADHA KUMAR.

YOU SHOULD GET MARRIED NOW. SHALL I FIND A BRIDE FOR YOU?

O QUEEN, I WILL FIND ONE MYSELF.

AND HE MARRIED AMARA DEVI, AN EXTREMELY INTELLIGENT GIRL OF A POOR FAMILY.

MAY YOU BOTH EVER PROSPER. I AM HAPPY FOR YOU.

THEY ARE PLEASED BY HIS CHOICE. NOW HIS STATUS WILL RISE FURTHER, WHILE OURS WILL DECLINE.

DO NOT WORRY. WE WILL HUMBLE AUSHADHA THROUGH HIS WIFE.

AND A FEW DAYS LATER, AFTER THE KING HAD RETIRED TO HIS BEDCHAMBER—

I WILL STEAL THE GEM FROM THE KING'S CROWN AND PLANT IT IN AUSHADHA'S HOUSE.

NOW TO FIX THE ARTIFICIAL GEM IN ITS PLACE.

WHAT A GENIUS I AM!

HEH! HEH! NOW FOR THE NEXT MOVE!

AH, MY BEAUTY! IT HURTS ME TO DROP YOU INTO THIS POT OF CURDS.

THEN SENAKA CALLED HIS MAID.

GO AND HAWK THIS IN THE STREET WHERE AUSHADHA LIVES.

BUT DO NOT SELL IT TO ANYONE EXCEPT AUSHADHA'S WIFE.

I UNDER-STAND, MASTER.

THE MAID SOON REACHED THE STREET WHERE AUSHADHA KUMAR LIVED.

CURDS! SWEET CURDS!

HEY WOMAN! LET ME SEE THOSE CURDS.

THE MAID PAID NO ATTENTION TO THE WOMAN.

HEY! I SAID I WANT TO BUY SOME CURDS.

CURDS! CREAMY CURDS!

DO YOU WANT TO SELL YOUR CURDS OR NOT?

STRANGE! WHY IS SHE HAWKING IF SHE DOES NOT WANT TO SELL?

CURDS! FRESH CURDS!

HEY WOMAN! DO YOU WANT TO SELL YOUR CURDS?

YES, MADAM.

HOW MUCH DO YOU WANT?

NOTHING.

BUT YOU MUST ACCEPT SOME MONEY.

NOT FROM YOU, O WIFE OF PANDIT AUSHADHA KUMAR.

THE MAID FORCED AMARA DEVI TO ACCEPT THE CURDS FREE.

WHY SHOULD SHE GIVE ME THE CURDS FREE?

QUICK, FOLLOW THAT WOMAN AND TELL ME WHERE SHE GOES.

MEANWHILE IN THE PALACE —

WHERE IS MY CROWN JEWEL? I SHALL HAVE YOU ALL BEHEADED.

MAHARAJ! PARDON ME. BUT...

...IT SEEMS TO BE THE WORK OF AN OUTSIDER.

NO OUTSIDER IS ALLOWED IN THESE QUARTERS.

THEY ARE, MAHARAJ! WHAT ABOUT US AND...

AND!

AND AUSHADHA KUMAR.

WHAT DO YOU MEAN?

ONLY THIS, MAHARAJ, THAT YOU SHOULD HAVE OUR HOUSES SEARCHED.

YOU MUST BE OUT OF YOUR MIND.

I AM NOT, MAHARAJ. I INSIST. BECAUSE WE SHOULD BE ABOVE SUSPICION.

THE HOUSES OF THE FOUR PANDITS WERE SEARCHED, OBVIOUSLY WITH NO RESULTS.

MEANWHILE, THE MAID SENT OUT BY AMARA RETURNED.

THAT WOMAN WENT STRAIGHT TO SENAKA PANDIT'S HOUSE.

OBVIOUSLY SENAKA SENT THIS POT OF CURDS. BUT WHY?

WHO IS IT?

SOLDIERS! OPEN THE DOOR.

A FEW HOURS LATER—

WE FOUND THE JEWEL MAHARAJ, IN AUSHADHA KUMAR'S HOUSE. IT WAS HIDDEN IN A POT OF CURDS.

VERY CLEVER!

VAIDEHA BECAME VERY UPSET. JUST THEN—

MAHARAJ, PANDIT AUSHADHA KUMAR WANTS TO MEET YOU.

I DO NOT WANT TO SEE HIS FACE.

SINCE VAIDEHA WAS NOT EVEN PREPARED TO LISTEN TO HIM, AUSHADHA DECIDED TO LEAVE THE CAPITAL.

I SHALL LIVE INCOGNITO IN A VILLAGE.

HE WENT TO A REMOTE VILLAGE WHERE NOBODY WOULD RECOGNIZE HIM.

GRANDPA, DO YOU NEED AN ASSISTANT?

YES, SON, I COULD DO WITH HELP.

AND HE STARTED WORKING AS THE POTTER'S ASSISTANT.

AFTER A FEW DAYS WHEN VAIDEHA HAD CALMED DOWN —

YOU DID NOT GIVE AUSHADHA A CHANCE TO EXPLAIN.

THE JEWEL WAS FOUND IN HIS HOUSE.

BUT THE ACCUSED MUST BE GIVEN A CHANCE TO DEFEND HIMSELF.

YOU ARE RIGHT. I SHALL DO THAT NOW.

A SEARCH PARTY SENT BY THE KING BROUGHT AUSHADHA KUMAR BACK TO THE COURT.

HOW DO YOU EXPLAIN THE RECOVERY OF THE CROWN JEWEL FROM YOUR HOME?

MY WIFE COULD TELL YOU.

WHEN AMARA DEVI WAS SUMMONED TO THE COURT—

MAHARAJ, THE GEM CAME TO OUR HOUSE IN THIS POT.

AND WHO BROUGHT THE POT TO YOUR HOUSE?

A VENDOR OF CURDS. I CAN HAVE HER BROUGHT HERE.

MAIDS! BRING HER IN.

THIS IS THE WOMAN WHO BROUGHT THE POT OF CURDS WITH THE GEM HIDDEN INSIDE.

PARDON ME, MAHARAJ, SENAKA PANDIT GAVE ME THE POT.

YOU, SENAKA?

I...ER...PLEASE PARDON ME, MAHARAJ.

NEVER! YOU SHALL BE SEVERELY PUNISHED.

BEING A BENEVOLENT SOUL, AUSHADHA KUMAR CAME TO SENAKA'S RESCUE.

PARDON HIM, MAHARAJ. IT WAS ONLY A PRANK.

YOU ARE NOBLE, AUSHADHA!

I APPOINT YOU COMMANDER OF MY ARMY.

I AM HONOURED, MAHARAJ.

SENAKA LEFT THE COURT A DEJECTED MAN.

WHATEVER I TRY RECOILS ON ME AND ONLY ADDS TO AUSHADHA'S GLORY.

BUT HE SOON RECOVERED AND DECIDED TO CHANGE HIS STRATEGY.

PANDIT AUSHADHA KUMAR, WHAT IS THE FIRST THING THAT A MAN SHOULD ACQUIRE?

THE TRUTH.

AND THEN?

WEALTH.

AND THEN?

MANTRA*

AND THEN?

THE ABILITY TO KEEP A SECRET.

FROM EVERYBODY!

YES! A SECRET SHOULD NOT BE DIVULGED TO ANYONE.

I HAVE GOT YOU AT LAST, AUSHADHA KUMAR!

MAHARAJ, AUSHADHA KUMAR IS UP TO SOMETHING.

SENAKA, STOP WORRYING. YOUR POSITION IS SAFE IN THE COURT.

I AM NOT WORRIED ABOUT MYSELF BUT ABOUT YOU.

ME! WHY?

BECAUSE I THINK AUSHADHA HAS SOME SECRETS WHICH HE WILL DIVULGE TO NO ONE.

I DON'T BELIEVE IT.

* WORDS HAVING MYSTIC POWERS

THE NEXT DAY AT THE COURT—

PANDIT AUSHADHA KUMAR, TO WHOM WOULD YOU CONFIDE YOUR SECRETS?

NO ONE.

NOT EVEN TO THE KING?

YES, NOT EVEN TO THE KING.

AFTER THE COURT WAS ADJOURNED—

THE COMMANDER OF MY ARMY IS SECRETIVE WITH ME! THIS IS AN ALARMING REVELATION INDEED!

DON'T WORRY, MAHARAJ. I WILL TAKE CARE OF THINGS.

MEANWHILE, AS AUSHADHA KUMAR RETURNED HOMEWARDS—

I HAVE NEVER SEEN THE KING LOOK SO PERTURBED.

THIS TIME SENAKA IS UP TO SOMETHING FAR MORE SERIOUS.

AUSHADHA KUMAR KNEW THAT SENAKA AND THE THREE OTHER PANDITS REGULARLY MET IN A SECLUDED CORNER OF THE GRAIN MARKET.

I HAD BETTER FIND OUT WHAT THEY ARE UP TO.

HE HID HIM-SELF IN A HEAP OF GRAIN AND WAITED.

SOON THE FOUR PANDITS ARRIVED.

I HAVE HATCHED A SECRET PLAN. WE SHALL HAVE AUSHADHA MURDERED.

WILL THE KING APPROVE OF OUR ACT?

HE WILL. BECAUSE I HAVE IMPRESSED UPON HIM THAT AUSHADHA HAS HIS EYES SET ON THE THRONE.

THIS SITUATION CALLS FOR DRASTIC ACTION.

AUSHADHA KUMAR GATHERED THE TROOPS AND SURROUNDED THE PALACE.

SEE THAT NO ONE ESCAPES.

AFTER ESTABLISHING HIS CONTROL OVER THE CITY, AUSHADHA KUMAR WENT TO MEET THE KING.

GLORY TO, KING VAIDEHA!

YOU HYPOCRITE! WHY DO YOU SHOUT MY PRAISES WHEN YOU ARE OUT TO DO ME HARM.

28

I HAVE NO INTENTION OF HARMING YOU, MAHARAJ. I JUST WANT TO MAKE YOU AWARE OF CERTAIN FACTS.

WHAT FACTS?

SENAKA PANDIT WANTED TO HAVE ME MURDERED.

?!

SO HE POISONED YOUR MIND TO GAIN YOUR SUPPORT.

ARE YOU WONDERING HOW I LEARNT YOUR SECRET, SENAKA?

YOU REVEALED IT TO ME YOURSELF BY SPEAKING OF IT TO OTHERS.

I THINK YOU WILL AGREE NOW THAT A SECRET SHOULD NEVER BE DIVULGED TO ANYONE. FOR...

...THE MOMENT IT IS DIVULGED IT CEASES TO REMAIN A SECRET.

AND, MAHARAJ, I ALSO WANTED TO PROVE THAT I WOULD EVER REMAIN FAITHFUL TO YOU.

EVEN AFTER I WRONGED YOU?

BUT YOU HAVE ALSO BEEN VERY KIND TO ME.

IT IS FORBIDDEN TO BREAK EVEN A BRANCH OF A TREE UNDER WHICH YOU HAVE TAKEN SHELTER...

...BECAUSE THEN IT HAS BECOME YOUR FRIEND. AND...

...IT IS A SIN TO WRONG A FRIEND.

HENCE I COULD NEVER EVEN DREAM OF HARMING YOU, MAHARAJ.

AUSHADHA, I AM SORRY THAT I FELL A PREY TO THE MALICIOUS PLOT OF SENAKA AND HIS HENCHMEN.

TO ATONE FOR THEIR SINS, THEY SHALL SERVE YOU AS SLAVES.

MAHARAJ, THEY WERE BLINDED BY THEIR SELFISH-NESS. WITH YOUR PERMISSION, I WOULD FREE THEM FROM THE BONDS OF SLAVERY.

PARDON US, AUSHADHA PANDIT. YOU ARE TRULY WISE AND NOBLE.

501 Krishna	580 Birbal the Inimitable	655 Anand Math
502 Hanuman	581 Raman the Matchless Wit	656 Adi Shankara
503 The Sons of Rama	582 Mahabharata	657 Vasantasena
504 Rama	583 Panchatantra –	658 Jahangir
505 The Gita	The Greedy Mother-in-law	659 Devi Choudhurani
506 Shiva and Parvati	584 Gopal the Jester	660 Ajatashatru
507 Nala Damayanti	585 Panchatantra - The Dullard	661 Kacha and Devayani
508 Chanakya	and other Stories	662 The Learned Pandit - Tales
509 Ganesha	586 Jataka Tales -	told by Sri Ramakrishna
510 Buddha	Stories of Wisdom	663 Aniruddha - A Tale
511 Savitri	587 Birbal the Genius	from the Bhagawat
512 Tales of Vishnu	588 Guru Gobind Singh	664 King Kusha - A Buddhist Tale
513 Hanuman to the Rescue	589 Krishna and Shishupala	665 The Deadly Feast -
514 Tales of Durga	590 Guru Nanak	A Jataka Tale
515 Ganga	591 The Syamantaka Gem	666 Kannagi - Based on a
516 Krishna and Rukmini	592 Ghatotkacha	Tamil Classic
517 Vivekananda	593 The Pandavas in Hiding	667 Bikal the Terrible - Folktales
518 Krishna and Jarasandha	594 Mahavira	from Madhya Pradesh
519 Elephanta	595 Sri Ramakrishna	668 The Acrobat - Buddhist Tales
520 Tales of Narada	596 Raja Bhoja	669 Ashvini Kumars -
521 Angulimala	597 Tales of Shivaji	Tales from the Vedas
522 Krishna and Narakasura	598 Vikramaditya's Throne	670 The Golden Mongoose
523 Raman of Tenali	599 Vishwamitra	671 The Cowherd of Alawi
524 Indra and Shibi	600 Kalidasa	672 The Priceless Gem -
525 Tales of Arjuna	601 Tales of Sai Baba	A Jataka Tale
526 Mahiravana	602 The Quick-Witted Birbal	673 Ayyappan
527 Bheema and Hanuman	603 Akbar	674 Vasavadatta
528 Kumbhakarna	604 Prithviraj Chauhan	675 Mangal Pande
529 Karttikeya	605 Padmini	676 Rana Kumbha
530 Shakuntala	606 Rani Durgavati	677 Magic Grove
531 Karna	607 A Bag of Gold Coins	678 Veer Savarkar
532 Sudama	608 Bhagat Singh	679 Swami Pranavananda
533 Abhimanyu	609 Friends and Foes - Animal	680 Fa Hien
534 Bheeshma	Tales from the Mahabharata	681 Amar Singh Rathor
535 Mirabai	610 Ravana Humbled	682 Tanaji
536 Ashoka	611 Babasaheb Ambedkar	683 Bahubali
537 Prahlad	612 Urvashi	684 Lachit Barphukan
538 The Churning of the Ocean	613 Soordas	685 Chand Bibi
539 Rani of Jhansi	614 Jataka Tales - True Friends	686 Chandra Shekhar Azad
540 Panchatantra - The Jackal	615 Jataka Tales -	687 Panna and Hadi Rani
and the War Drum	Stories of Courage	688 Bimbisara
541 The Lord of Lanka	616 Jataka Tales -	689 Tripura
542 Draupadi	Tales of Misers	690 Lalitaditya
543 Jataka Tales -	617 Jataka Tales -	691 Hiuen Tsang
Monkey Stories	The Hidden Treasure	692 Veer Hammir
544 Subhas Chandra Bose	618 Birbal to the Rescue	693 Jayaprakash Narayan
545 Birbal the Wise	619 Jataka Tales - Nandivishala	694 Guru Tegh Bahadur
546 Vali	620 Hitopadesha - How	695 Nahusha
547 Garuda	Friends are parted	696 The Historic City of Delhi
548 Rabindranath Tagore	621 Udayana	697 Chandrahasa
549 Tales of Shiva	622 The Tiger and the	698 Ram Shastri
550 Sati and Shiva	Woodpecker	699 Jagadis Chandra Bose
551 Tulsidas	623 Kabir	700 Jawaharlal Nehru
552 Tansen	624 Dayananda	701 Noor Jahan
553 Jataka Tales - Jackal Stories	625 Battle of Wits	702 Nachiketa and other
554 Jataka Tales -	626 The Pandava Princes	Tales from the Upanishads
Elephant Stories	627 Harsha	703 Tales of Yudhisthira
555 Jataka Tales - Deer Stories	628 Ramana Maharshi	704 Jallianwala Bagh
556 Hitopadesha - Choice of	629 Uloopi	705 Bappa Rawal
Friends	630 Rana Sanga	706 Sakshi Gopal
557 Birbal the Witty	631 Chaitanya Mahaprabhu	707 The Tiger-Eater
558 Birbal the Clever	632 Vidyasagar	708 Subramania Bharati
559 Birbal the Just	633 Tales of Maryada Rama	709 Jagannatha of Puri
560 Panchatantra - How the	634 Chandragupta Maurya	710 The Fearless Boy and other
Jackal ate the Elephant	635 Amrapali	Buddhist Tales
561 Panchatantra -	636 Krishnadeva Raya	711 The Celestial Necklace
Crows and Owls	637 Yayati	712 Andhaka
562 Panchatantra -	638 King Shalivahana	713 The Fool's Disciples
The Brahmin and the Goat	639 Krishna and the False	714 The Queen's Necklace
563 Rana Pratap	Vasudeva	715 Ramanuja
564 Shivaji	640 Paurava and Alexander	716 The Adventures of
565 Drona	641 Gopal and the Cowherd	Agad Datta
566 Surya	642 Shah Jahan	717 Baladitya and Yashodharma
567 Indra and Shachi	643 Ratnavali	718 Basaveshwara
568 Vikramaditya	644 Gandhari	719 Chandralalat
569 Malavika	645 Lokamanya Tilak	720 Kapala Kundala
570 Dasharatha	646 The Pandit and the Milkmaid	721 Rash Behari Bose
571 Dhruva and Ashtavakra	- Tales told by	722 Megasthenes
572 Ancestors of Rama	Shri Ramakrishna	723 Jnaneshwar
573 Jataka Tales – Bird Stories	647 Lal Bahadur Shastri	724 Bagha Jatin
574 Jataka Tales -	648 Samudra Gupta	725 Sultana Razia
The Magic Chant	649 Tales from the Upanishads	726 Ranjit Singh
575 Jataka Tales -	650 Mahatma Gandhi -	727 Raja Raja Chola
The Giant and the Dwarf	The early days	728 Deshbandhu Chittaranjan
576 Jataka Tales -	651 Baddu and Chhotu	Das
The Mouse Merchant	652 Aruni and Uttanka - Tales	729 Bajirao
577 Harishchandra	from the Mahabharata	730 Shrenik - Jain Tales
578 Kesari, the Flying Thief	653 Jayadratha	731 Ellora Caves - The Glory
579 Madhvacharya	654 Tales of Balarama	of the Rashtrakootas

ILISA, THE GILDMASTER

ILISA, THE GILDMASTER, HAD MORE MONEY THAN HE COULD EVER SPEND, BUT HE WAS TIGHT-FISTED.

I'VE STAYED OUT LONGER THAN I SHOULD.

I HOPE MY WIFE HAS NOT BOUGHT ANYTHING FOR HERSELF IN MY ABSENCE. SHE IS SO EXTRAVAGANT.

AND AS FOR MY WORTHLESS CHILDREN, ALL THEY CAN THINK OF IS EATING.

IF I DIDN'T KEEP A CONSTANT WATCH ON THEM THEY WOULD EAT ME OUT OF HOUSE AND HOME.

HELP A HUNGRY MAN, SIR.

OUT OF MY WAY, YOU WRETCH!

YOU WON'T GET A THING FROM ME!

YOU WANT TO GIVE AWAY WEALTH?

YES, MAHARAJ. HOARDED WEALTH IS OF NO USE TO ANYONE.

YOU MAY DO SO.

THE GREATEST MISER IN THE LAND WANTING TO GIVE AWAY HIS WEALTH! WELL, WELL!

WONDERS WILL NEVER CEASE!

THE MAN THEN WENT TO ILISA'S HOUSE.

THERE'S A STRANGER IN TOWN IMPERSONATING ME.

HE HAS TAKEN LEAVE OF HIS SENSES, BUT I'D BETTER BUY SOMETHING FOR MYSELF BEFORE HE CHANGES HIS MIND.

SOON, PEOPLE BEGAN TO STREAM INTO ILISA'S HOUSE.

MASTER... MASTER...

COME IN, COME IN.

PICK UP WHATEVER YOU WANT AND GO.

WHATEVER WE WANT!

OUT OF MY WAY!

HE MAY CHANGE HIS MIND ANY MOMENT.

YES, WE ALL KNOW WHAT A MISER HE IS.

ONE MAN WORKED MORE METHODICALLY THAN THE OTHERS. INSTEAD OF RUSHING INTO THE HOUSE, HE CHOSE A BULLOCK-CART FOR HIMSELF...

...LOADED IT WITH VALUABLES FROM THE STOREROOM...

...AND DROVE AWAY SINGING THE PRAISES OF HIS BENEFACTOR.

THERE IS NO ONE GREATER THAN THE NOBLE ILISA!

I'VE GOT A FINE PAIR OF BULLOCKS, AND A CARTLOAD OF TREASURE.

MAY ILISA LIVE A THOUSAND YEARS!

WHAT!

SOMEONE'S PRAISING ME!

I WONDER WHO IT IS.

THERE IS NO ONE GREATER THAN ILISA!

THANK YOU, MY GOOD MAN!

?

I CAN SEE THAT YOU ARE A GOOD JUDGE OF MEN.

YOU ARE RIGHT.

I JUST HAVE TO LOOK AT A PERSON TO KNOW...

MY BULLOCKS!

MY CART! AND MY BELONGINGS!

YOU ARE ALL GOING TO PAY DEARLY FOR THIS!

I'LL COME BACK WITH THE KING'S MEN.

ILISA RUSHED TO THE PALACE.

MAHARAJ, I AM BEING LOOTED!

PEOPLE ARE CARRYING AWAY MY PROPERTY!

BUT GILDMASTER...

...YOU YOURSELF CAME HERE AND ASKED FOR MY PERMISSION TO GIVE AWAY YOUR WEALTH!

I!

MAHARAJ, HAVE YOU EVER KNOWN ME TO GIVE AWAY ANYTHING?

SOME IMPOSTOR HAS TAKEN MY PLACE!

I WILL HAVE HIM BROUGHT HERE.

WHEN THE IMPERSONATOR WAS BROUGHT TO THE PALACE, THE KING AND HIS COURTIERS FOUND THEMSELVES GAZING AT TWO MEN WHO LOOKED IDENTICAL IN ALL RESPECTS.

NOW WHO IS WHO?

MY WIFE COULD IDENTIFY ME, MAHARAJ.

BUT WHEN ILISA'S WIFE WAS BROUGHT TO THE PALACE AND ASKED TO IDENTIFY HER HUSBAND—

THAT'S MY HUSBAND!

UNGRATEFUL WOMAN! AFTER ALL I'VE DONE FOR YOU!

NOW WHO... WHAT... WHY, MY BARBER OF COURSE!

MAHARAJ, MY BARBER COULD IDENTIFY ME!

THE BARBER WAS BROUGHT TO THE PALACE AND ASKED TO IDENTIFY ILISA.

I'LL HAVE TO EXAMINE THEIR HEADS, MAHARAJ.

THIS IS UNCANNY!

I CANNOT IDENTIFY THE GILDMASTER, MAHARAJ.

WHAT DO YOU MEAN!

I HAVE A WART ON MY HEAD. HAVE YOU FORGOTTEN?

YOU HAVE A WART... BUT SO DOES HE!

EVEN MY WIFE HAS IDENTIFIED HIM AS HER HUSBAND!

I'LL BE THROWN OUT OF MY OWN HOUSE... AND I'LL LOSE ALL MY WEALTH... OOOH!

HE HAS FAINTED!

THROW SOME WATER ON HIM.

WHEN ILISA WAS RESTORED TO HIS SENSES—

I SHALL NOT FRIGHTEN YOU ANY MORE.

I AM YOUR FATHER... COME DOWN FROM HEAVEN.

F-FATHER!

ALL THE WEALTH YOU POSSESS IS MINE. I WAS GENEROUS TO THE POOR AND NEEDY...

...BUT YOU HAVE PUT ALL MY WEALTH UNDER LOCK AND KEY AND IT IS OF NO USE TO ANYONE!

I WILL TAKE AWAY ALL MY WEALTH IF YOU PERSIST IN SUCH BEHAVIOUR!

I... I WON'T, FATHER!

GIVE ME ANOTHER CHANCE!

THEN ILISA'S FATHER RETURNED TO THE CELESTIAL WORLD...

...AND ILISA RETURNED HOME...

...A GENEROUS AND CONSIDERATE MAN.

KESIYA

LONG AGO, THERE LIVED A MISER KESIYA. HE WAS THE KING'S TREASURER. ONE DAY AS HE WAS GOING HOME—

HE'S EATING POODAS.

IT'S SUCH A LONG TIME SINCE I HAVE EATEN POODAS.

I COULD ASK MY WIFE TO MAKE SOME...BUT THE COST !

WHEN KESIYA REACHED HOME—

YOU LOOK SAD. WHAT'S THE MATTER?

NOTHING.

IN FACT, I'LL MAKE ENOUGH FOR THE WHOLE NEIGHBOURHOOD!

WHAT!

HAVE YOU TAKEN LEAVE OF YOUR SENSES, WOMAN!

I... I...

ALL RIGHT, I'LL MAKE JUST ENOUGH FOR US.

FOR US?

FOR THE CHILDREN, FOR YOU AND FOR ME.

LEAVE THE CHILDREN OUT.

THEY MAY NOT CARE FOR POODAS.

THEN I'LL MAKE JUST ENOUGH FOR THE TWO OF US.

YOU DON'T REALLY WANT TO EAT POODAS, DO YOU?

ER... WELL...

I THOUGHT AS MUCH. MAKE JUST ENOUGH FOR ME.

WAIT!

WE MUST BE CAREFUL. IF YOU MAKE THE POODAS IN THE KITCHEN, THE AROMA WILL ATTRACT THE NEIGHBOURS...

...AND THEN WE'LL HAVE TO GIVE THEM SOME. I'LL TELL YOU WHAT WE'LL DO.

WE'LL TAKE EVERYTHING WE NEED UP TO THE TERRACE AND YOU CAN MAKE THE POODAS UP THERE.

SO KESIYA AND HIS WIFE, CARRIED THE UTENSILS AND INGREDIENTS REQUIRED TO MAKE THE POODAS...

MAKE A SMALL ONE FOR HIM.

BUT KESIYA'S WIFE FOUND THAT SHE COULD NOT MAKE A SMALL POODA FOR THE UNINVITED GUEST.

THAT'S TURNED OUT EVEN BIGGER.

I CAN'T HELP IT!

THE PASTE KEEPS ON SPREADING OVER THE WHOLE PAN. THERE'S SOMETHING VERY STRANGE GOING ON HERE.

YOU'RE JUST A BAD COOK, THAT'S ALL!

GIVE HIM THAT ONE ON TOP AND LET HIM GO AWAY.

THEY ARE ALL STUCK TOGETHER.

SIT AND EAT.

I WANT THEM NOT FOR MYSELF...

...BUT FOR MY LORD BUDDHA AND HIS DISCIPLES. THEY ARE WAITING FOR ME.

BUDDHA!

F-FORGIVE ME! I DID NOT KNOW...

COME WITH ME IF YOU WISH TO MEET HIM.

THE MONK RAISED HIS HAND AND A STAIRCASE APPEARED.

KESIYA AND HIS WIFE WENT DOWN IT...

...TILL FINALLY—

HERE WE ARE.

THE LORD BUDDHA.

BUDDHA ACCEPTED THE OFFERING OF POODAS AND THEY WERE DISTRIBUTED AMONG HIS MONKS.

KESIYA AND HIS WIFE TOO GOT THEIR SHARE.

THIS IS THE FIRST TIME I HAVE SHARED MY FOOD WITH STRANGERS.

AND STRANGELY, I FEEL HAPPY... ER, WHAT ARE YOU STARING AT?

THE POODAS.

EVERYONE HAS EATEN BUT THE TRAY IS AS FULL AS BEFORE.

NEVER HAVE I SEEN SUCH A WONDER! THIS IS THE GREATEST DAY OF MY LIFE!

KESIYA RETURNED HOME A CHANGED MAN.

WIFE, TOMORROW YOU WILL MAKE POODAS FOR THE WHOLE NEIGHBOURHOOD.

MANDUKA– THE LUCKY ASTROLOGER

ONE DAY A POOR BRAHMANA WAS PASSING BY THE HOUSE OF A MERCHANT.

*FROG

THAT'S WHAT I'VE BECOME, A MANDUKA! AND I'M TIRED OF IT.

?!

I WISH I COULD DO SOMETHING··· ANYTHING··· WHICH WOULD MAKE EVERYONE···

···SIT UP AND TAKE NOTICE OF ME.

HEY, I'VE GOT IT!

THE BRAHMANA RAN BACK···

···TO THE PLACE WHERE THE WEDDING WAS GOING ON···

···AND QUIETLY LED AWAY THE HORSE ON WHICH THE BRIDEGROOM HAD COME.

COME IN, COME IN, SIR.

HOW WELL MY PLAN IS WORKING! ALREADY I'M BEING TREATED AS AN HONOURED GUEST.

YOUR SERVANTS TELL ME YOU HAVE LOST A HORSE.

THAT'S RIGHT.

I SHALL REWARD YOU HANDSOMELY IF YOU CAN HELP US FIND HIM.

GIVE ME A FEW MOMENTS AND I SHALL TELL YOU EXACTLY WHERE HE IS.

I'LL HAVE TO STUDY THESE CHARTS AND... AND... AH!

YOU'LL FIND THE HORSE NEAR THE STREAM. BUT MAKE HASTE, HE IS IN DANGER OF BEING STOLEN.

RUSH TO THE STREAM!